J.D.C.A.PRIDEAUX

THE ENGLISH NARROW GAUGE RAILWAY

A PICTORIAL HISTORY

D1556146

David & Charles
Newton Abbot · London · North Pomfret (Vt) · Vancouver

British Library Cataloguing in Publication Data
The English narrow gauge railway.
   1. Railroads, Narrow-gauge—England—
History—Pictorial works
   I. Prideaux, J. D. C. A.
385'.5'0942   HE3820
ISBN 0-7153-7511-3
Library of Congress Catalog Card Number 78-52160

Set in 10 on 11pt Compugraphic English
and printed in Great Britain
by Biddles Limited, Guildford
for David & Charles (Publishers) Limited
Brunel House   Newton Abbot   Devon

Published in the United States of America
by David & Charles Inc
North Pomfret   Vermont 05053   USA

Published in Canada
by Douglas David & Charles Limited
1875 Welch Street   North Vancouver   BC

Contents

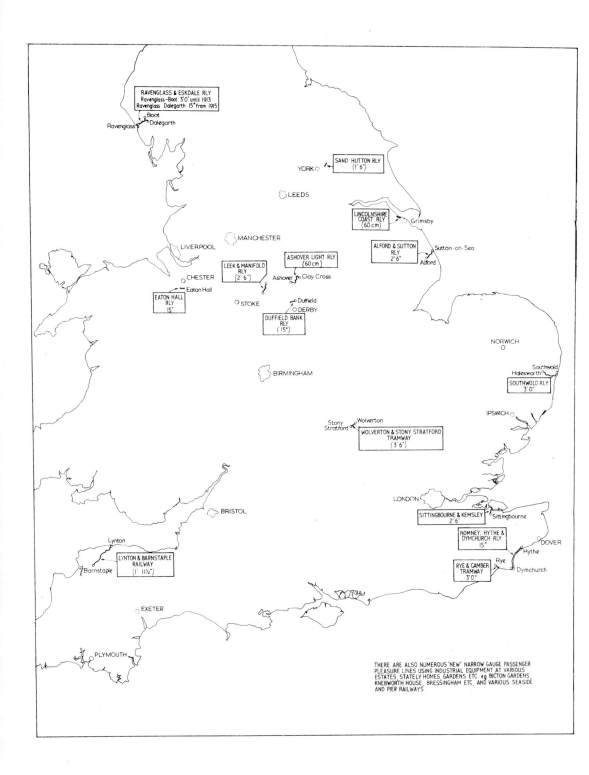

RAVENGLASS & ESKDALE RLY
Ravenglass–Boot 3'0" until 1913
Ravenglass Dalegarth 15" from 1915

Boot
Ravenglass Dalegarth

SAND HUTTON RLY
(1' 6")

YORK

LEEDS

LINCOLNSHIRE
COAST RLY
(60 cm)

Grimsby

LIVERPOOL

MANCHESTER

ALFORD & SUTTON
RLY
2' 6"

Sutton-on-Sea
Alford

LEEK & MANIFOLD
RLY
(2' 6")

ASHOVER LIGHT RLY
(60 cm)

Ashover   Clay Cross

CHESTER

Eaton Hall

EATON HALL
RLY
15"

STOKE

Duffield

DERBY

DUFFIELD BANK
RLY
(15")

NORWICH

BIRMINGHAM

Southwold
Halesworth

SOUTHWOLD RLY
3' 0"

IPSWICH

Stony
Stratford   Wolverton

WOLVERTON & STONY STRATFORD
TRAMWAY
(3' 6")

LONDON

BRISTOL

SITTINGBOURNE & KEMSLEY
2' 6"   Sittingbourne

DOVER

ROMNEY, HYTHE &
DYMCHURCH RLY
15"   Hythe

Rye
RYE & CAMBER
TRAMWAY
3' 0"   Dymchurch

Lynton

L'YNTON & BARNSTAPLE
RAILWAY
(1' 11½")

Barnstaple

EXETER

PLYMOUTH

THERE ARE ALSO NUMEROUS 'NEW' NARROW GAUGE PASSENGER
PLEASURE LINES USING INDUSTRIAL EQUIPMENT AT VARIOUS
ESTATES, STATELY HOMES, GARDENS ETC eg BICTON GARDENS,
KNEBWORTH HOUSE, BRESSINGHAM ETC, AND VARIOUS SEASIDE
AND PIER RAILWAYS

Introduction

Railways were invented in England. Development was rapid and competitive, producing from the opening of the Stockton & Darlington Railway in 1825 to the Grouping almost a century later several hundred independent concerns. Branch lines were promoted as much to protect territory (or penetrate a rival's area) as to serve local demand. As a result, the country, particularly in the more prosperous areas, was covered by a dense network of standard gauge railways which left little room for a substantial secondary network of the sort which evolved in many continental countries.

The English narrow gauge railway has, therefore, always been a rarity. It was, and remains, exclusively rural. As such it was built to serve one of four purposes: first, it could provide the transport necessary for mineral workings; second, it could connect a town to the nearest standard gauge railway; third, it could be an agricultural railway; and fourth, it could be built for pleasure in its own right or to carry pleasure seekers.

The Ravenglass & Eskdale was the first English narrow gauge railway, opened in 1875. The concept was taken, ready formed, from Wales where such lines were not only well established but were taken very seriously as prototypes for the colonial networks then under consideration. Like the Welsh lines, the R&ER was a mineral railway, built in this case to carry iron ore from the hills of Cumberland to the standard gauge at Ravenglass. Its gauge, 3ft, was the narrow gauge 'standard' of the time, also used for various lines in Ireland and the Isle of Man. As a mineral railway it was a singular disaster. While it managed to carry about as much traffic in its first year as one of the less successful Welsh systems, the mines soon failed, leaving it to subsist on what local traffic there was. There was very little. The railway declined slowly until arrears of maintenance became too pressing—and then quietly closed a year or two before the first world war. Mineral railways have not, in fact, played a major part in English narrow gauge history, though the Ashover, one of the last to be built, did fall into this category. There were also such lines as the Snailbeach, and numerous narrow gauge quarry and industrial railways, but they were purpose built for a particular and local industrial function. In no sense were they public railways, common carriers or passenger lines, such as most of the lines described here.

Most of the lines opened during the 19th century connected a town bypassed by the main line railways to some convenient point on the standard gauge. The first such line was the Southwold in Suffolk, opened in 1879 and linking the seaside town of Southwold to the Great Eastern Railway at Halesworth. Traffic grew slowly until by 1900 the railway was carrying about 100,000 passengers and 15,000 tons of freight a year. This led to abortive schemes to convert the railway to standard gauge, but even with this level of traffic the railway was scarcely able to renew its equipment and provide a return on investment.

One of the schemes for a railway to Southwold which failed, planned the line as a roadside tramway. This was quite a sensible option provided that the country was fairly flat. Such 'tramways' only differed from normal narrow gauge railways in using existing roads to provide a right of way; they were built to carry both freight and passengers and should not be confused with town tramways. Two lines were built in this way during the 1880s. The first was the Alford & Sutton in Lincolnshire which connected Sutton-by-Sea to the Great Northern at Alford. Unfortunately the standard gauge reached Sutton within two years and, stripped of most of its traffic, the tramway was soon closed. It was open for only five years between 1884 and 1889. The 3ft 6in gauge Wolverton & Stony Stratford was a little more successful, lasting in all for 40 years from 1886 to 1926. It originally linked Wolverton LNWR (with its railway works and main line station) to Stony Stratford, and was then extended across the Great Ouse to Old Stratford and to Deanshanger to serve an agricultural implement manufacturer. Part of the extension was built as a 'normal' railway, using bull-head

Above: The Ravenglass & Eskdale was the first English public narrow gauge railway, opening to freight in 1875 and to passengers the next year. Its traffic soon failed however, and the line settled down to a precarious existence. This very early photograph shows *Nabb Gill*, one of two small 0-6-0Ts, at Boot with the third class coach. At this stage the equipment was still sound and in good condition. Note the archaic smokebox door.

L&GRP

Below: The Southwold opened soon after the Ratty, but did a quite different job, connecting the town of Southwold to the standard gauge at Halesworth. This photograph shows the junction station, with 2-4-0T No 3 *Blythe* arriving on the 10.15 from Southwold in September 1910.

K. A. C. R. Nunn

track on an embankment, which indicates how tenuous the distinction between narrow gauge railway and tramway could become. Transhipment of parcels was avoided by a piece of pure Victorian ingenuity. The parcels wagons 'were fitted with wheels having adjustable flanges', which it seems were in sections and could be withdrawn inside the tread surface so that the wagons could also run on the normal road surface. The only problem was that no one seems to have asked themselves whether two or three miles of rail haul justified so much trouble. The parcels service did not prosper and the wagons were soon scrapped. The Rye & Camber followed ten years later. Called a tramway, it was in fact a railway and the first pleasure line, serving the golf course and beach at Camber.

The Lynton & Barnstaple reverted to first principles. Its promoters made it quite clear that it was modelled on the most successful Welsh line—the Festiniog—and it adopted the Welsh gauge of 1ft 11½in rather than 2ft 6in—3ft 6in previously used in England. Like the Southwold and Sutton lines it linked a coastal town to the standard gauge. However the country it traversed was very different from the flat lands of eastern England. The steep-sided valleys of Exmoor provided a setting for a very fine, and very English railway. Its equipment was excellent without being elaborate, and needed to be pretty good. Well over half the line was graded at 1 in 50 and engines had to work hard in both directions. Fine Staffordshire countryside was just as much in evidence along the Leek & Manifold Railway opened in 1904, six years after the L&B, but this 2ft 6in line was remarkable in serving no settlements of any size. It was really an agricultural line, built to 'open-up' country in the Peak District foothills and to help a scattered population bring their produce to Leek market. It had two remarkable features. First, the locomotives and rolling stock were to an Indian design, and second it was the first railway to use transporter wagons to carry standard gauge wagons on to the narrow gauge, thus avoiding transhipment.

The purpose-built agricultural railway in England took on a rather different form. In the late Victorian period the great estates dominated the countryside, and it was not therefore surprising that agricultural railways would be associated with great houses. The prototype was at Duffield Bank, the home of Sir Arthur Percival Heywood. The grandson of a Manchester banker his roots were in the industrial revolution rather than in landowning, and he seems to have been drawn to things mechanical from an early age. He became the first person to take a first in Applied Science at Cambridge but seems to have been reluctant to become a professional engineer. Despite (or perhaps because of) Britain's industrial pre-eminence, engineering was socially rather inferior, and Arthur Heywood settled at Duffield and looked for ways in which to become an amateur engineer. Like many other people at the time he was impressed by the way in which the Festiniog managed to handle some 150,000 tons a year on a gauge of 1ft 11½in, and he set out to see how far he could further reduce the gauge while maintaining stability. The premise was the smaller the gauge the cheaper the railway, and he wanted to find a railway which would be economic for traffic levels of only 5000 tons a year. In modern terms that is about one large lorry load a day, five days a week. He opted for a gauge of 15in, and set about perfecting track, locomotives and rolling stock. The basic premise was based on an oversimplification—very little money is necessarily saved by reducing the gauge below 2ft, while carrying capacity falls rapidly. M. Decauville, a Frenchman, who developed portable railways for agricultural and military use in a much more pragmatic and entrepreneurial fashion, rapidly increased his gauge from 40cm (1ft 4in) to 60cm (1ft 11⅝in). However, sound or flawed as the concept may have been, Arthur Heywood developed his 15in gauge with great style and laid out a demonstration line in his grounds. Many people visited it, and many were clearly impressed, but the agricultural railway boom just never happened. Heywood's railways arrived at the same time as the long agricultural depression which was to last until the second world war. Yet whatever failings Heywood's ideas had as a system there is no doubt that Heywood and his railways played an important part in the development of narrow gauge and miniature railways in later years.

One working Heywood railway, however, was built in 1896, some 20 years after Heywood had started work. By this stage the Duke of Westminster had already spent some £600,000 on turning his early nineteenth century mansion at Eaton into something which accorded better with late Victorian ideas of what a Gothic house should be. So £6,000 for a railway to connect his house and the estate works to the standard gauge three miles away must have been chickenfeed. Heywood built the railway for him and it did its job well for 50 years. Only one other real agricultural railway followed. Again it was built for a very wealthy man and in this case one suspects that the motive was

Leek & Manifold Valley Railway 2-6-4T No 2 *J. B. Earle* on trial train at Hulme End before the opening of the line. E. R. Calthrop was the line's engineer but his main interests as an engineer were in India, and the locomotives and rolling stock mirrored Barsi Light Railway practice. The line only reached Leek over a standard gauge link from Waterhouses, and indeed the navvy who opinioned 'it's a grand bit of line, but they wanna mak a go on it for it starts from nowhere and finishes up at the same place' proved prophetic. *L&GRP*

at least partly pleasure. The Sand Hutton line opened in 1920 by which time the lorry was already available. Despite this it carried a quite respectable traffic of up to 13,000 tons a year, but lasted only 12 years. The 18in gauge was determined by the second-hand stock used.

If Heywood's ideal of an estate railway scarcely took root, then his demonstration of the pleasures to be obtained from a railway in the garden certainly did. In Edwardian years several country houses acquired railways, and many of the locomotives came from the Northampton firm of Bassett-Lowke. Built for pleasure, these locomotives were scale models, and very different from the practical narrow gauge engines designed by Heywood. The 15in gauge provided a good base for quarter scale locomotives, and Bassett-Lowke built the first of what was to become a famous series of 4-4-2s in 1905. The Eaton Railway was the trial ground, and, thereafter, engines started to appear in the grounds of exhibitions and on seaside amusement lines. Promotion came from Bassett-Lowke and from an associated company calling itself Narrow Gauge Railways Ltd. This development came of age in an extraordinary way. The first world war had curtailed the seaside business, and stopped the use of such railways to carry people round exhibitions abroad. NGR Ltd discovered the Ravenglass & Eskdale, by now quite derelict, leased it and promptly set about converting it to 15in gauge. Equipment was a mixture of Heywood and scale-model stock. It was a bold venture, and, against all odds, it succeeded. The railway won a Royal Mail contract and instituted year-round passenger services. It proved more economical than horse and cart for local freight traffic, and in 1922 a granite quarry opened which was to provide the 15in gauge line with the steady bulk traffic denied to its 3ft gauge predecessor.

One of the people who had bought a Bassett-Lowke scale model was J. E. P. Howey. His engine was tried at Eaton and eventually went to Ravenglass. After the first world war he became more ambitious. He had inherited a substantial part of the city of Melbourne, in Australia, and so could indulge his hobbies. He went motor racing, and together with his equally well-off rival Count Zborowski decided to build a railway against their retirement. Zborowski died in a racing accident, but not before they had had some scale locomotives built, and had tried one of them out at Ravenglass. Howey toyed with the idea of buying the Ravenglass & Eskdale, thought of extending it to Windermere, and then decided that the line was too far from London. Eventually he settled on Romney Marsh, and opened a line from Hythe to New Romney in 1927, with an extension to

Dungeness the following year. It was a very expensive way of running a light railway. It was double track which ensured that the 15in gauge was not being used for economy. Further model type locomotives were more expensive both in first cost and maintenance than a narrow gauge engine of equivalent power—and the railway was very generously equipped with them. In all events the railway must have given its owner (and passengers) much pleasure, and filled a transport need into the question. During the second world war it remained busy, carrying troops, the Pluto oil pipes and even an armoured train.

While these developments were taking place on the Ravenglass and the Romney the earlier lines were rapidly shutting up shop. The Ravenglass (in its first form) and Alford & Sutton had of course closed before 1914. Once the first world war was over other lines followed them. The Wolverton & Stony Stratford suspended services in 1920, and it was only a takeover by the London & North Western which kept it going until 1926, when the LMS closed it. The Southwold followed in 1929, Sand Hutton in 1932, Leek & Manifold in 1934 and Lynton & Barnstaple in 1935. The railways, always marginal, could not survive once there was any effective road competition. The Rye & Camber last ran in 1939; by the time the war was over it just did not seem worth repairing it. The Eaton Hall and Ashover, both freight only, ran their last trains in 1946 and 1950 respectively.

This left just the two 15in gauge lines, at Ravenglass and Romney. Beckfoot Quarry, which provided the Ravenglass with its basic traffic closed in 1952. The railway was opened by quarrying interests and they could not be expected to run it indefinitely. The railway was finally sold at auction in 1960. The purchasers were Mr Colin Gilbert and the Ravenglass & Eskdale Railway Preservation Society. J. E. P. Howey died in 1963 and the Romney's future remained in doubt until it was bought by a consortium of notable railway enthusiasts. Tourists make up the vast majority of travellers today, yet both railways manage to run winter services as well. The Ratty, for such is the R&ER affectionately known, operates one train a day up the valley. Largely for the benefit of its own staff, it is nevertheless welcome as an addition to local public transport.

There has also been something of a new narrow gauge mania. The 2ft gauge Lincolnshire Coast Light railway started operations in 1960 and provides a Rye & Camber-ish service to a holiday camp site. Two industrial lines have seen new life. The 2ft 6in gauge Sittingbourne & Kemsley was a papermill railway in Kent while the 2ft gauge Leighton Buzzard Narrow Gauge Railway runs round the outskirts of the town using the tracks of a railway laid out in the 1920s to avoid the damage caused by carrying the local sand by road. And a narrow gauge railway has become an accepted tourist attraction at great houses, gardens and zoos, with new lines such as those at Knebworth, Bicton, Bressingham gardens, Whipsnade and elsewhere, mostly using former industrial and quarry railway equipment. Is it not ironic that the estates which had no use for Sir Arthur Heywood's railways 100 years ago should be so interested in them now?

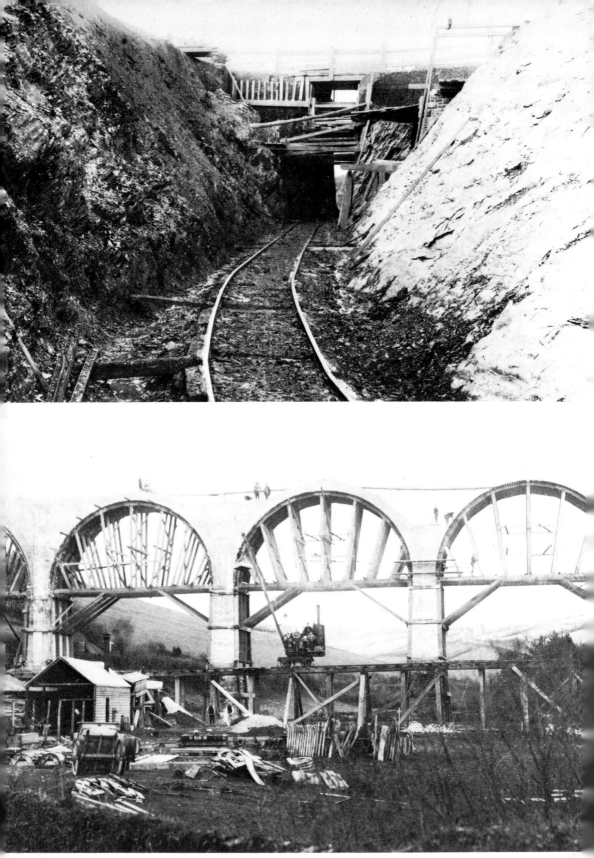

1 CONSTRUCTION

Left: The construction period was possibly the most important in any of the railways' lives, and also the least photographed. Luckily two railways, the Lynton & Barnstaple and Romney, Hythe & Dymchurch kept albums showing what the lines looked like while they were being built. This photograph, of a bridge of the Lynton & Barnstaple, illustrates what a mucky business it usually was.　　　　*North Devon Atheneum*

Below left: Chelfham Viaduct was the major engineering work on any of the lines. Construction is traditional with brick arches built round falsework. It was high enough to need a steam crane to hoist the marland bricks to the bricklayers.　　　　*North Devon Atheneum*

Below: The concrete age had arrived by the time the RHDR was built — and the techniques used to built the 'tunnel' under the main road at New Romney would not seem entirely unfamiliar today.　　　　*RHDR*

Left: Pomp and Ceremony. Bratton on the Lynton & Barnstaple on 11 May, 1898. The parish council celebrated the opening by erecting a triumphal arch and presenting an address to the railway's Chairman, Sir George Newnes. *Bratton Fleming VHC*

Above: Inagural train of the last major line: 4-8-2 No 5 leaves Hythe on the Romney, Hythe & Dymchurch Railway, 16 July, 1927.

Below: There were just too many guests for the two coaches available on the Leek & Manifold's opening day, as this photograph at Hulme End shows. *L&GRP*

2 OPENING

Summer, autumn and winter, the railway's basic
function was to serve the local population, a task
exemplified by these three photographs of Beckfoot.
R&ER

3 A TRAIN FOR ALL SEASONS

Devon arrives at Ravenglass with all the passenger stock. By the time this photograph was taken — early this century — things had gone a long way downhill. The locomotive had been patched up by Lowca Engineering Works, and sported continuous brakes and new safety valves, but the general condition of the track indicated how little maintenance there was. Passenger services finally ceased in 1908 and freight trains ran on an occasional basis until some time in 1913.   *L&GRP*

Poverty did at least bring out the English genius for improvisation. At Miteside a local farmer and landowner provided his own station, in a style which could only really be described as nautical vernacular. He is reputed to have used the train regularly for his journey up the valley — but to have been reluctant to pay for his collie to accompany him. The dog, it is said, always had to wait for both train and master at destination!

D. Brough Collection

Southwold 2-4-2T No 1 *Southwold* waits to leave
Halesworth in January 1920.   *K. A. C. R. Nunn*

Blythborough, looking towards Southwold circa 1890.
The station was not ready until three months after the
railway opened, indicative of the fact that the traffic
potential of intermediate villages was hardly central to
the line's justification. The small timber goods shed on
the left, came two years later in 1881, and belonged to
Odams manure stores.

After leaving Blythburgh the railway climbed through pine woods where herons nested.

Before reaching its destination the line crossed the river Blyth on a swing bridge. The bridge shown here was replaced with a stronger one in 1908 during a time when it seemed that the line might be rebuilt to standard gauge. The new bridge was, however, a white elephant, and it was last swung for navigational purposes in 1914. The Southwold Railway was not the first form of 19th century transport to die in Suffolk.

THE SOUTHWOLD EXPRESS :-

THE GOODS TRAIN LEAVES HALESWORTH HALF AN HOUR TOO SOON - THUS MEETING THE 2.20. FROM SOUTHWOLD
BETWEEN BLYTHBURGH AND WENHASTON - AFTER MUCH DISCUSSION THE DRIVERS DECIDE TO FIGHT FOR THE RIGHT
OF THE ROAD - A SPORTING PASSENGER MAKES THE MOST OF THE SITUATION - THE GUARD WAITS ANXIOUSLY.

The line was subject to the usual witticisms—in this
case recorded in a series of humorous postcards by
Reg Carter. The Company's rules exude a fine
pomposity; it took upon itself the right to imprison its
drivers for up to two years for the more serious
misdemeanours—which must have made it fair game.

THE SOUTHWOLD EXPRESS·

THE GUARD GOES BIRDSNESTING & THINKS AN EGG IN THE NEST IS WORTH TWO IN
THE EYE -   N B THE SPEED LIMIT IS STRICTLY OBSERVED ON THIS LINE.

Left: Two early photographs at Southwold itself. The shrubs on the platform in the photograph of No 3 *Blyth* waiting to depart for Halesworth are actually horse chestnut trees and help in dating views of the station. Later photographs also show a lot more building. The photograph of No 1 *Southwold* (*bottom left*) is the only known photograph of the first engine to carry the name—which was returned to the builders in 1883 whence she finally found her way to Columbia and outlasted her sisters by a few years.

Below: Tram engine No 1 on a mixed train at Alford, circa 1885. Photographs of the Alford & Sutton Tramway are few and far between, since the line was only open between 1884 and 1889. Like the Southwold it linked a seaside town (Sutton) to the local main line railway—in this case the Great Northern. Unlike Southwold, Sutton soon gained its own standard gauge railway and this quickly took the freight and much of the passenger traffic. *Nainby*

Stony Stratford is two miles east of the London & North Western main line at Wolverton, and a tramway was opened in 1886 to link the two towns and, particularly, to provide transport for men working in the railway shops at Wolverton. This very Victorian photograph of Stony Stratford shows one of the original Krauss steam tram engines.

V. Goldberg Collection

The line was extended—partly on ordinary railway track—for a further 2½ miles to Deanshanger. However for some reason it did not succeed and passenger services ran only for a year or so. This is in fact the only photograph the author has ever seen of the extension.

D. Brough Collection

Two further photographs taken at Stony Stratford and showing (*above*) a Green condensing tram engine, and also (*below*) the Bagnall 0-4-0ST bought in 1922 after the line had been taken over by the LNWR. This must be very near the end: the engine is lettered LMS and the line finally closed in 1926.   *Both V. Goldberg Collection*

Overleaf: The Lynton & Barnstaple was considerably the longest of the English narrow gauge lines, and in many people's minds the finest. A pre-opening trial train poses at Collar Bridge where the climb from the Yeo Valley really started.   *North Devon Atheneum*

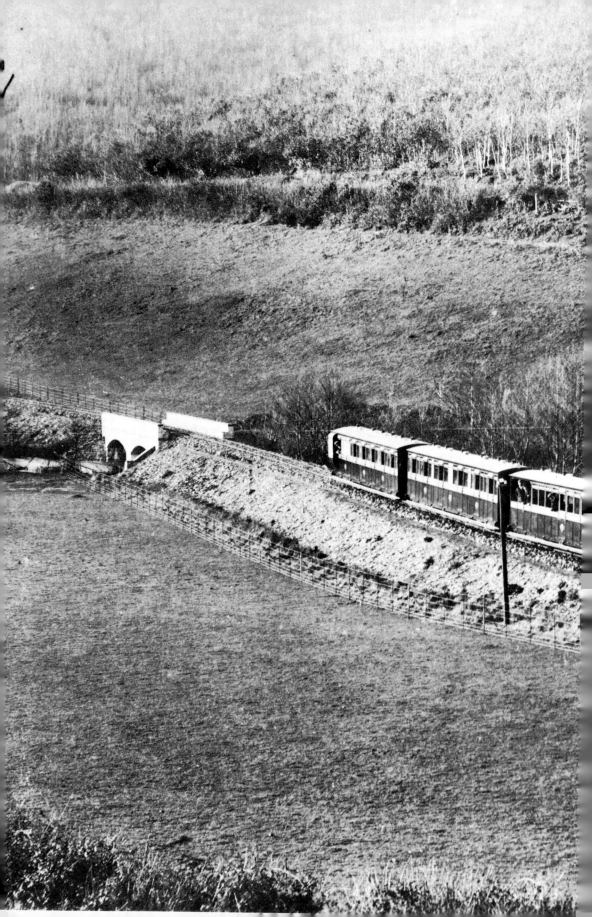

Top left: Summer evening idyll. *Taw* drifts down into Lynton with the sun just catching the tops of the trees in the West Lyn Valley far below.   *The Times*

Above: Steam and smoke. The last train crossing Chelfham Viaduct. The climb from Collar Bridge was a continuous 1 in 50, and nine coaches represented the maximum load for two engines.

Left: Lew on an up train near Caffyns Halt in July 1935.
S. W. Baker

Left: When the Leek & Manifold Railway opened, its standard gauge feeder was not ready, and a temporary terminus was provided at Waterhouses as shown here (*top*). Connection with Leek was at first maintained by two North Stafford Railway steam buses—one of which is shown outside the Inn at Waterhouses (*bottom*).
L&GRP

Below: The junction between the standard gauge from Leek and the Leek & Manifold was at Waterhouses. The standard gauge was on the right and at a slightly higher level. The number of platform barrows seems excessive, even allowing for the milk churns which were one of the line's few staple traffics. *L&GRP*

Minimum cost railway. The Rye & Camber was built without benefit of any formal procedure such as an Act of Parliament. Its capital was all of £2,300 and it opened three months after incorporation. Its basic function was to connect the town of Rye with its newly opened golf course. The first locomotive was a diminutive (6 ton) Bagnall 2-4-0T *Camber*, seen here at Rye station in 1909. *H. L. Hopwood*

Rye Station consisted of a collection of undistinguished corrugated iron sheds. It was some way from the town across the River Rother near the Folkestone road and the railway had to resort to paint to make sure potential patrons noticed it at all. The locomotive in this picture is *Camber's* stable mate, *Victoria*, built two years later and marginally bigger; both the railway's coaches are also shown. By the early 1930s a small petrol tractor had taken over from the steam locomotives and the operating staff reduced to one man. *H. L. Hopwood*

Despite the tramway title the railway was a fully fenced
line running on its own right of way and not alongside a
road. Here *Victoria* approaches Rye on the 1.45 p.m.
from Golf Links on 18 July, 1914. Golf Links station was
the terminus until 1908 when the line was extended to
Camber Sands. Golf Links station served the links, and a
ferry. One of the idiosyncrasies of the line was the
special 2d return for 'Golf Caddies and Dogs'.
K. A. C. R. Nunn

Apart from the two coaches the line's rolling stock
consisted of a few small wagons and later two open
coaches. Bearings were covered to try to protect them
from the sand as far as possible.   *K. A. C. R. Nunn*

Top left: Sir Arthur Heywood with his first locomotive *Effie* at Duffield Bank, around 1875. Sir Arthur set out to find the smallest gauge capable of being practically and advantageously worked — and decided that 15in was the minimum for stability. Thereafter the advocacy of 15in gauge railways for military, agricultural and industrial use became a hobby and something of a crusade.

L&GRP

Bottom left: Heywood did not claim to be starting entirely from scratch. In particular he admired C. E. Spooner's work on the Festiniog, and took due note of the 18in 'shop railways' which had developed at such places as Woolwich, Chatham and Crewe. These could be pretty extensive. The Woolwich line ran to 55 track miles, and handled some 2000 tons daily as well as a half-hourly passenger train service. This photograph shows Hudswell Clark 0-4-0ST *Culverin* of 1884 with a saloon coach at Woolwich around 1920. Some equipment from the Woolwich Arsenal line survives at Bicton.

Major E. W. Taylerson

Above: Every detail of a proper minimum gauge line was fully developed and tried out in Sir Arthur's own workshops and on the demonstration line in the grounds of Duffield Bank. This became well known, but it was 20 years before anyone built a 15in gauge line on the principles he so strenuously advocated. This was at the Duke of Westminster's estate of Eaton Hall in Cheshire. Sir Arthur laid out and equipped the Eaton Hall Railway as a more workaday example of his ideas. This photograph taken in June 1904, shows the engine shed at Duffield Bank, with two Duffield locos *Ella* and *Muriel* on shed, and the second Eaton engine *Shelagh*, then brand new, under trial. *F. Wilde, courtesy M. Jacot*

4 MINIMUM GAUGE RAILWAY

The 19th century house was a great deal more than a large house in beautiful surroundings. It was usually the focus of a large estate, and as these houses grew increasingly large and as coal replaced wood as the normal fuel, ceased to be anything like self-sufficient. The first railway the Author knows of laid down to take fuel to the house was the Belvoir Castle Railway — in 1815. Horse drawn, it survived in relative obscurity for a century. Of more interest to our story was the Eaton Hall Railway, built by Sir Arthur Heywood for the Duke of Westminster and opened in 1896. This fine photograph, presumably taken very early on, since *Katie* has yet to receive her nameplates, shows the engine shed at Belgrave Lodge.   *F. Wilde*

5 THE ESTATE RAILWAY

Map and gradient profile of the Eaton Railway.

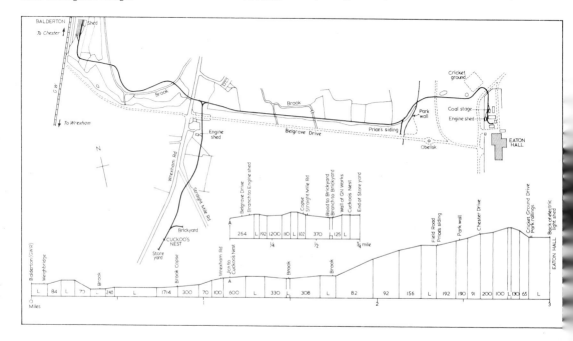

The main traffic was coal to the Hall, returning with empty wagons. These two photographs show respectively, 0-4-0T *Katie* (*above*) and the later and rather larger 0-6-0T *Shelagh* (*below*).   *L&GRP; F. Wilde*

Overleaf: High summer. *Shelagh* with both passenger coaches. Many distinguished people visited the line, often riding on the trains laid on to carry guests to shoots on the estate. These included Sir Winston Churchill, as well as British and foreign royalty. *F. Wilde*

Top left: On an average day the railway's work consisted of a trip light to the Hall, a return run to Balderton and then 'as required' at the estate works at Cuckoo's nest. *Katie* poses with the open coach at the works. *F. Wilde*

Above: From 1922 until the line's closure in 1946 the Heywood locomotives were largely replaced by a Simplex tractor, shown here at Balderton. *L&GRP*

Bottom left: A cold spell meant increased coal consumption at the Hall, and therefore more work for the railway. *Shelagh* struggles with a snow clearing train — the plough is attached to the tool truck. Both the plough and the brake van are now at New Romney. *F. Wilde*

Top: Despite Sir Arthur Heywood's efforts the Eaton Railway was not emulated for many years. Not until 1920 did another fully fledged estate railway appear — at Sand Hutton. This was started on the 15in gauge already used for the garden railway at the house. However, while still under construction 18in gauge War Department stock came up for sale. This solved the rolling stock problem, and three locomotives and 75 wagons were quickly bought, thus determining the gauge. Seen here is one of the Hunslet 0-4-0WTs used on the line — with its WD number. *H. G. W. Household*

Above: The Sand Hutton railway was Sir Robert Walker's pride and it did not long survive his death. It was a well thought out agricultural light railway. Freight traffic was quite good, running to 13,000 tons a year. Claxton Lane was the most elaborate agricultural station. *H. G. W. Household*

Top right: The locomotive shed was some way away at Sand Hutton itself. In the railway's better days two engines were steamed daily. *H. G. W. Household*

Centre right: Passenger traffic was always light, with a maximum annual total of only just over 2000. Yet a commodious composite coach was provided, seen here at White Sike Junction. The entrances were soon modified, for someone, no doubt, got a very sore head! *Catchside*

Right: No 12 near Sand Hutton Central in 1927. The altered coach entrance is apparent. *H. G. W. Household*

Top left: While Eaton Hall acquired its railway for the serious purpose of transporting goods to the house and to serve the estate workshops, other country house owners built railways — usually of smaller 10 ¼ or 9 ½ in gauge and thus miniature railways rather than narrow gauge — purely and simply for their own enjoyment. Any actual work, like the hay train shown here on the Broome Railway was quite incidental!   *J. T. Holder*

Bottom left: The 15in gauge was used as a reasonably accurate base for quarter full size scale models. As such, the locomotives were very different from the Heywood machines such as *Shelagh* which was built for daily heavy haulage. However the gauge was the same, and two famous trials took place at Eaton. In June 1905, the first Bassett-Lowke Atlantic *Little Giant* proved to be capable of hauling five tons at a maximum speed of 26mph. The photograph is at Belgrave engine shed.   *F. Wilde*

Above: In the final summer before the first world war the largest miniature locomotive then built came to Eaton. *John Anthony* belonged to J. E. P. Howey and was about twice as big as *Little Giant*. Built for the house Mr Howey had then leased, she was stored at Eaton Hall until 1916 when she was sold to the newly opened Ravenglass & Eskdale and renamed *Colossus*.
RHDR

6 PRIMARILY FOR PLEASURE

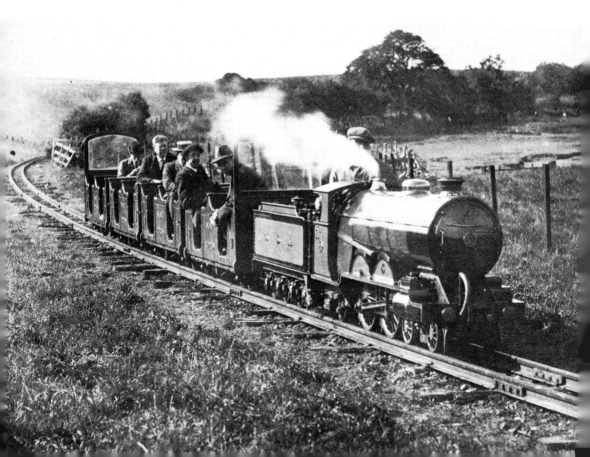

eft: Probably the most extraordinary event in English ɜrrow gauge history was the lease of the Ravenglass & ʒkdale by Narrow Gauge Railways Ltd in July 1915, ɜnd conversion of the line to 15in gauge. The ɾrangements were, however, illegal, for the line's ɾiginal Act authorised any gauge between 3ft and ɜandard—but not 15in, and negotiations took place ith only one creditor of an incorporated company. ɾoreover the arrangement took place in the middle of a ʳorld war. To work the line the new 'owners' brought ɜ a Bassett-Lowke 4-4-2, *Sans Pareil,* which was idle ʜter Norwegian exhibition work, together with some ʝur-wheeled open carriages from the same source, and ʜew vehicles from Duffield Bank which Sir Arthur was ʒrsuaded to sell. These two photographs taken that ʳst year show, (*top*), *Sans Pareil* at Ravenglass (note e 3ft gauge siding still in situ and the very hastily ɥd track on which the train is standing, devoid of some ɜh plates) and, (*bottom*), on the short stretch of track ɥse up to Muncaster Mill. *R&ER*

Above: The next two locomotives arrived from Eaton. *Katie* was sold as soon as the last Heywood locomotive *Ursula* arrived, and *John Anthony* was taken out of mothballs at Belgrave and renamed *Colossus.* This photograph shows *Katie* at Ravenglass in those very early days, on a train made up entirely of Heywood stock. The old loading bank is behind the engine and one of the scale models is backing down into the station. *Bassett-Lowke*

Overleaf: Operations were very casual, being based more on seaside funfair than on railway practice. *Sir Aubrey Brocklebank* heads an up train approaching Irton Road with a second portion following 'on sight'.

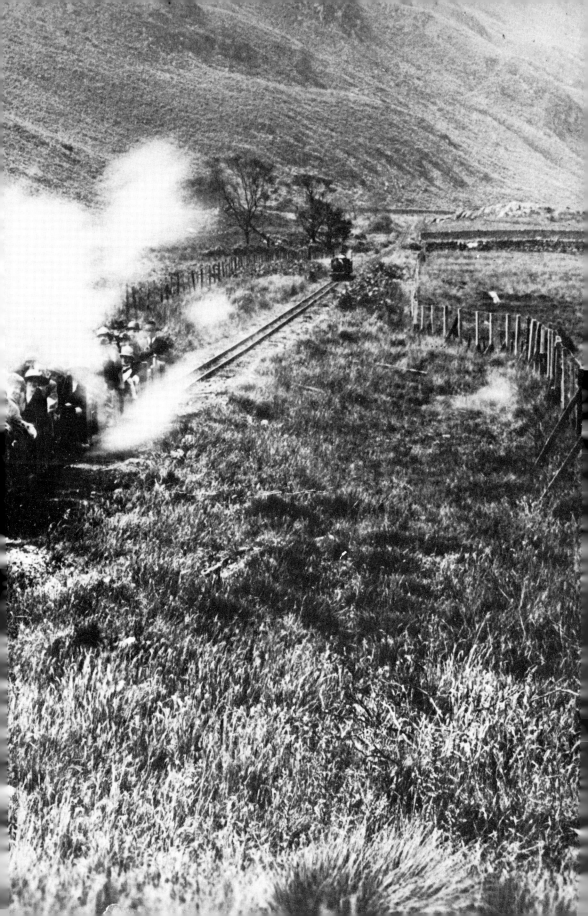

Left: The carefree approach comes out again in this delightful photograph. The gauge narrowing was generally achieved by moving the rails inwards on the old sleepers, and the original 3ft gauge fastenings were often left in situ.   *Bassett-Lowke*

Above: At rest. *Sir Aubrey Brocklebank* in Ravenglass shed.   *Mary Fair*

Left: Transhipment at Balderton in 1905. The crate contains *Little Giant*, surely one of the more unusual loads to need transfer from standard to narrow gauge.

Bassett-Lowke

Above and below: The stone traffic at Ravenglass produced arrangements for undersized wagons which could well be described as pernickety.

Both H. G. W. Household

7 TRANSHIPMENT

Bottom left: Warthill on the Sand Hutton in 1927. It is quite a well thought out arrangement, with a high level narrow gauge siding on the right so that loads could easily be transferred to the standard gauge, and a low level siding on the left to transfer traffic the other way.

H. G. W. Household

Transhipment avoided. The Leek & Manifold's greatest claim to fame is that of being the first narrow gauge line to use transporter wagons to carry standard gauge wagons over the narrow gauge. The first photograph on this page shows No 1 *E. R. Calthrop* at Redhurst crossing, on a train which includes two transporters.

L&GRP

In the second photograph, taken in 1930 at Waterhouses, the engine has just positioned a transporter up to the standard gauge stop block and the guard is releasing the wagon brake and wheel clamps before running the wagon off the transporter. The rail, seen lying against the wagon wheels, was a late modification introduced when the transporters started to be used to carry milk tanks. It raised the standard gauge wagon further off the transporter, clearing its brake gear.

L&GRP

Until roads were improved — normally in the late 1920s in the remote districts served by narrow gauge lines — the railways carried what local traffic there was. These delightful photographs of the Ravenglass & Eskdale illustrate the diversity of local traffic — including even Lord Rea's car at Eskdale Green on its way to Ravenglass and repair. The locomotive is 4-6-2 *Colossus*.   *Mary Fair*

8 THE LOCAL RAILWAY

Farm produce provided more usual traffic. Potatoes are loaded into standard Heywood wagons at Irton Road, while both *Ella* and the farmer's horse wait patiently.
Mary Fair

No doubt the railway was particularly appreciated in bad weather. Passengers board a down train at Eskdale Green on an iron icy day.
Mary Fair

Winter passenger services depended on the Royal Mail contract, which, in Ratty's case was held until 1927/28. Traffic was light, and an internal combustion locomotive was used whenever possible for economy. *Lizzie*, the railway's weird and wonderful Model T Ford, complete with chicken coop cab, leaves Irton Road.   *Mary Fair*

Left: Things did not always go smoothly, especially when the engine was being turned on its built-in turning plate. Still, everyone including the postman seems ready to lend a hand.   *Mary Fair*

Bottom left: John Porter, the Eskdale Green postman, employed in more usual fashion, unloading mail sacks at Irton Road. Carrying mail was yet another task for the standard Heywood wagon. Sir Arthur stressed flexibility and designed the wagon bodies so that they could easily be lifted off and the wagon used as a flat truck for carrying timber, rails (and even cars).   *Mary Fair*

Below: Christmas mail at Irton Road 1925. If the weather was really bad the train would be worked by a steam engine — or even two as in this festive scene. The locomotives are *Muriel* and *River Esk* and the coach came from the original 15in gauge garden railway at Sand Hutton. It was the lightest closed coach on the line.   *Mary Fair*

The Ashover Light Railway opened to freight in 1924 and to passengers in April 1925. Built to the 60cm (1ft 11⅝in) gauge to use surplus (and very cheap) first world war military equipment, its main traffic was limestone and fluorspar from Fallgate to Clay Cross. Passenger traffic was quite heavy that first year, when 63,657 passengers were carried. It was down to less than half that within two years, and never recovered. *Peggy* on the 3.50 p.m. from Clay Cross near Chesterfield Road on 30 August 1925. *K. A. C. R. Nunn*

Top right: Hummy at Ashover in 1931. The year-round passenger service was dropped in 1930. It was further restricted to three days a week from 1932 and was entirely abandoned in 1936. *L&GRP*

9 LATECOMERS

Peggy at Clay Cross in 1925. The line had six steam locomotives, all similar Baldwin 4-6-0Ts built in 1916 and 1917 for war service with the British Army. *K. A. C. R. Nunn*

Bottom right: Bridget taking water at Fallgate in 1936. *L&GRP*

ADVICE OF DESPATCH OF GOODS.

FROM

DAVEY, PAXMAN & CO., LTD.,

STANDARD IRON WORKS.

TELEGRAMS: PAXMAN, COLCHESTER.
TELEPHONE No. 52 (2 LINES) COLCHESTER.

To The ROMNEY, HYTHE & DYMCHURCH
RAILWAY,
New Romney,
Kent.

July 19th...1927.

The goods mentioned below have been sent forward on **to-day**

From **Colchester** *By* **L.& N.E.Rly.,** *Carriage* **forward**

Consigned to **NEW ROMNEY STATION, S. Rly.**

16042 & 16044,

Two 15" Gauge Locomotive Engines and Tenders.
"SAMSON" and "HURRICANE"

Bolted on rails as before and loaded side by side on
special FLAT TRUCK No. N.E. 761602.

each engine Tons 5 -4 -0 -0.
"   tender "   1 -13-0- 0.

For DAVEY, PAXMAN & Cº Limited

Top left: Although it opened only two years after the Ashover, with a gauge only 8½ in narrower, the Romney, Hythe & Dymchurch was about as different from the Ashover as it could be. It was (and is) a passenger line, with little freight traffic, and was built as much for its owner's pleasure as to serve a transport need. Rails were the only equipment bought cheap after first world war use. It was laid out as a miniature main line with double track and to 15in gauge. The railway belonged to Capt J. E. P. Howey, one time owner of *John Anthony*, and its first locomotives were ready before the railway was even started. *Green Goddess* was therefore tried out on the Ravenglass & Eskdale; the photograph shows her en route from Davey Paxman's works at Colchester.   *RHDR*

Above: The railway was clearly fun, and attracted distinguished visitors even while it was under construction. The Duke of York (later King George VI) drove a train from New Romney to the children's holiday camp he supported at St Mary's Bay on 5 August, 1926. The Duke can be seen on the footplate, accompanied by Capt Howey (who usually wore a hat to conceal his bald patch), while Nigel Gresley, Chief Mechanical Engineer of the London & North Eastern Railway, whose Pacifics provided the prototype for the Romney engines, sits nonchalantly on the tender.

RHDR

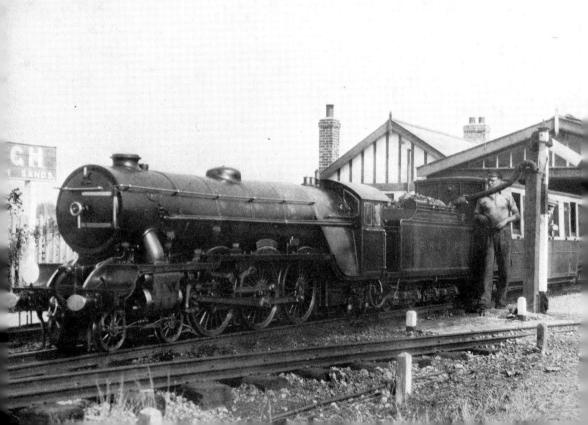

Top left: Comparisons with the LNER Pacifics gave useful publicity, and made quite a point about size. *Typhoon* and LNER 4472 *Flying Scotsman* at Kings Cross Shed. *RHDR*

Left: One of the two three-cylinder RHDR Pacifics taking water at Dymchurch in the early days. The coach is also notable for it was very comfortable and with steam heating; it was a positive attempt to attract off-season traffic. *RHDR*

Above: This rare photograph showing non-passenger traffic was also taken at Dymchurch — three milk churns! *RHDR*

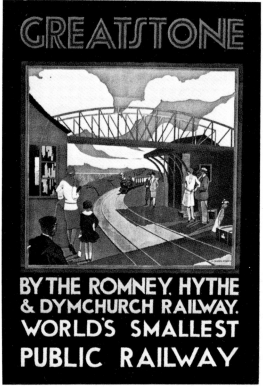

GREATSTONE

BY THE ROMNEY, HYTHE & DYMCHURCH RAILWAY. WORLD'S SMALLEST PUBLIC RAILWAY

Above: War service. The Romney ran along the South Kent coast where German invasion troops were expected in 1940. It was commandeered by the Army, and heavily used for troop transport, and later to help in construction of the Pluto flexible cross Channel pipeline project after the D-day invasion in 1944. Moreover it had the world's one and only 15in gauge armoured train. It has been claimed that it did shoot down a German aircraft. The railway was certainly bombed on several occasions.   *Imperial War Museum*

Top left: The RHDR started life with an ample stock of locomotives – five 4-6-2s, two 4-8-2s and *The Bug*, an 0-4-0TT. In 1931 two more 4-6-2s arrived, this time of Canadian appearance, and *The Bug* left shortly afterwards for Belfast. *The Bug* was little used once construction was complete, but this photograph does show it outside New Romney shed. Note the large headlamp fitted to *Typhoon* for working evening trains.   *D. Brough Collection*

Left: Gentleman's light sporting locomotive – the Rolls Royce petrol locomotive on a winter train at New Romney about 1935. The locomotive was built from Capt Howey's 1914 Silver Ghost as an economical machine for winter traffic which was always light, and only survived since Howey supported his railway from his pocket.   *Lens of Sutton*

DUNGENESS
BY THE ROMNEY, HYTHE AND DYMCHURCH RAILWAY
THE WORLDS SMALLEST :: PUBLIC RAILWAY ::

Above: Permanent way is one of the great railway misnomers. It is not at all permanent but needs continuous effort. Platelayers at work on the Ratty in the 1920s with Muncaster Fell in the background. Old 3ft gauge sleepers have been dug out and are dumped on the right. The ballast looks very poor.   *Mary Fair*

10 WAY AND WORKS

Top right: By contrast, the text book view of what 15in gauge track should be like. Sir Arthur Heywood's specification for the Eaton Railway. The photographs shown elsewhere in the book suggest that very high standards were indeed maintained.   *L&GRP*

Right: Track was not very different on the wider gauges Rail weight was usually in the range 25-40 lb/yd — and light rail was not necessarily associated with very narrow gauge. The Ravenglass & Eskdale used the 40lb rail provided for its 3ft gauge predecessor, and rails of up to 56 lb/yd were used for the 18in gauge line at Woolwich. The Southwold on the other hand used only 30 lb/yd rail. This photograph shows resleepered and reballasted track on the Lynton & Barnstaple in the 1920s. The original 40 lb/yd rails, some 30 years old at the time, were re-used.   *H. G. W. Household*

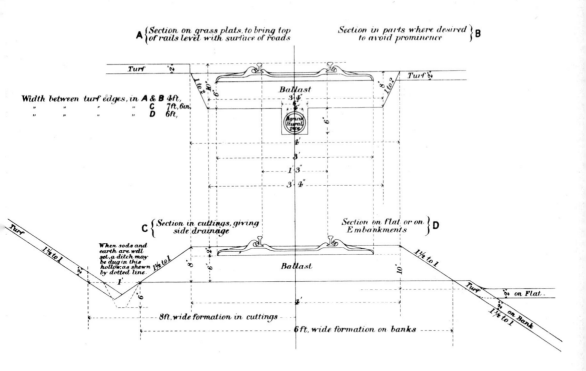

A { Section on grass plats, to bring top of rails level with surface of roads

Section in parts where desired to avoid prominence } B

Turf

Turf

Ballast

3' 4"

Width between turf edges, in **A & B** 4ft,
" " " " **C** 7ft, 6in,
" " " " **D** 6ft,

1 to 2

0' 6"

1 to 2

6"

4'

3'

1' 3"

3' 4"

C { Section in cuttings, giving side drainage

Section on flat or on Embankments } D

Turf

1½ to 1

6"

When sods and earth are well set, a ditch may be dug in this hollow, as shewn by dotted line

1'

6"

1½ to 1

8"

6"

Ballast

10'

1½ to 1

Turf

½ on Flat.

1½ to 1

½ on Bank

4'

8ft, wide formation in cuttings

6ft, wide formation on banks

Cross Sections of Eaton Railway.

Above: Stations varied greatly, An overall roof, like that shown here on the first Ravenglass station, gives the advantage of allowing the station to double as a carriage shed. This is a very old railway practice recently revived by the RHDR for its new station at New Romney. This historic photograph was taken during the trials of *Green Goddess* in 1925, and shows Greenly on the engine step and Howey standing behind the cab.

RHDR

Top right: Sand Hutton Central could only be described as an oversized garden shed. *H. G. W. Household*

Right: Bridgeworks were avoided wherever possible. The most impressive were Chelfam viaduct on the Lynton & Barnstaple, illustrated on pages 10 and 27, and the Southwold swing bridge shown on page 18. Duke of York's bridge was the major work on the Romney, but was comparatively minor at 60ft long. The train is the 3pm from Hythe, the locomotive No 6 *Sampson*, and the date, 31 August, 1949.

K. A. C. R. Nun

Above: On the L&B, Blackmoor, Woody Bay (shown here) and Lynton were quite elaborate stations. They were described as being in Swiss Chalet style.
S. W. Baker

Top right: Greenly designed a consistent set of buildings for the RH&D, in similar style to the bogus half-timbered houses then going up throughout the Southern commuter belt. Several are illustrated elsewhere, and New Romney was the largest. Like the rest of the railway they were built to last 40 years, and so many have now been replaced. This is the main office building fronting the original terminus at New Romney.
RHDI

Right: The overall roof at Hythe, photographed in 1966. Note the gantry carrying the then new colour-light signals.
G. M. Kichensid

Previous page: A bank holiday train at Beeston Tor on the Manifold in the early days. Traffic as heavy as this was not necessarily profitable as it was often heavily peaked; indeed it is said that in one year the Manifold carried more passengers in Wakes week than in the whole of the rest of the year. At least the Manifold improvised rather than acquiring expensive assets which only sat idle for the rest of the year. All four passenger coaches are in use, plus both open wagons which have been fitted with temporary roofs, and three transporters where there are seats but no roofs. There is even a transporter with a coal wagon on at the back.

L&GRP

Above: A later Manifold holiday train, with both engines in steam and three transporters in use as open coaches.

L&GRP

Right: Crowds, in this case at Barnstaple Town on the L&B. The last L&B train was a summer excursion such as this.

11 HIGH SUMMER

Below: The Lynton & Barnstaple went out of its way to accommodate the tourist, and provided eight special observation coaches. No 2 shown here, was one of a pair of brake coaches with a solidly comfortable 1st class saloon leading to an open observation platform. No improvisation here!

L&GRP

Above: Summer traffic was of course the main reason why the Romney, Hythe & Dymchurch was built at all. Scenes such as this with crowds of excited children are as common today as they were when this photograph was taken at New Romney in the early 1930s.   *RHDR*

Top right: No 9 *Winston Churchill* blows off as it approaches Hythe alongside the Royal Military Canal on a summer afternoon in 1950.   *K. A. C. R. Nunn*

Right: Three of the RHDR 1927 12-seat Clayton 'Pullmans' as running in the 1960s; in body style they were reminiscent of Gresley LNER coaches.
    G. M. Kichenside

LUGGAGE ONLY

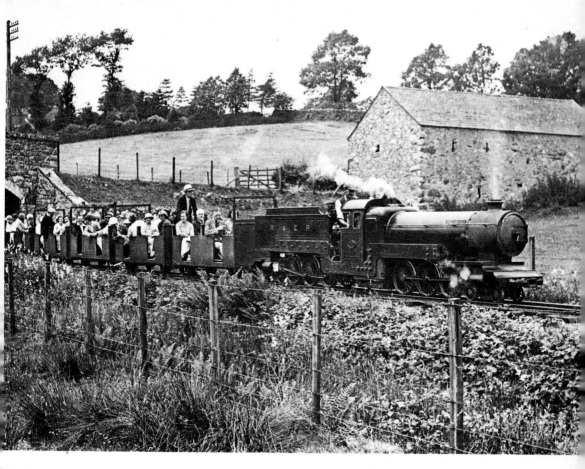

Top left: Devon staggers into Irton Road with all the Ravenglass passenger stock, and four wagons used as extra coaches, on Whit Monday 1906.   *Mary Fair*

Above: Parts from both locomotives were used with a new boiler to build the modified Fairlie *River Mite*, seen leaving Eskdale Green in 1933. Although it was a brave attempt at a powerful locomotive, the frames, wheels, bearings and motion from the scale models were not really up to heavy regular work and the engine was dismantled after a short life.   *Mary Fair*

Left: As traffic on the Ravenglass grew during the 1920s the scale model engines were increasingly used in tandem. *Colossus* double heads *Sir Aubrey Brocklebank* in 1927 — their last year of operation.
          Mary Fair

Top left: Few English narrow gauge lines had significant originating mineral traffic. At Ravenglass the iron ore traffic for which the line was built failed very early on, but a granite quarry was developed at Beckfoot from 1922 and provided 10,000-20,000 tons a year, the railway's staple traffic. The quarry face at Beckfoot is shown in 1928 with one of the railway's three Fordson tractors in the foreground, and *Muriel's* old boiler behind, being used to provide power for the drills.

Mary Fair

Above: Joan at Stretton on the Ashover, with six loads of limestone and one passenger coach. The fireman is returning from closing the crossing gates. The Ashover carried far and away the most mineral traffic.   *L&GRP*

2 MINERAL RAILWAY

Bottom left: The need for economical motive power to haul the year-round stone traffic provided a stimulus for developing internal combustion locomotives. Here, CL 1, known variously as the Ford or *Bunny*, shunts at the quarry in 1925.   *Mary Fair*

Below: No other railway relied on mineral traffic to the extent of the Ashover or the Ravenglass. However the Romney carried quite a lot of shingle used for building work, especially just after the war, and the Sand Hutton's main traffic was bricks. Clayton Brickworks, shown here, were well equipped and only failed when the reserves of clay ran out.   *H. G. W. Household*

Top left: An attractive feature of the Ravenglass (and the Romney) in recent years has been the occasional gatherings of 15in gauge locomotives from many lines. In 1976 Ravenglass was the locale, and this photograph of the engine shed shows from the left Krupp 4-6-2 *Rosenkavalier* from Bressingham (one of three similar locomotives, built for the Munich exhibition of 1938, two of which are now at Bressingham and one on the Romney), *River Mite, Northern Rock* and *River Irt.* The narrow gauge proportions of *Northern Rock* and *Irt* contrast very noticeably with the scale size engines.
R&ER

Bottom left: The shape of things to come? Another visitor, *Sian* from the Fairbourne in Wales, passes Muncaster Mill, now owned by the railway and restored to working condition. The engine performed very well, and as the Ratty has a small four-coupled engine from Dundee awaiting conversion to 15in gauge, the eventual result may not be dissimilar.
R&ER

Above: River Irt while still in miniature form near Beckfoot. Snow is not uncommon in Cumbria at Easter, but, even so, one passenger has chosen to travel in the open coach.
R&ER

13 TODAY

Below: A works train in the woods. While neither the Ratty nor the Romney ever closed, the previous administrations had allowed them to run down. Unspectacular but vital work on formation and track demands much effort and money. Either railway would welcome support — addresses are given in the tables at the back of the book.
R&ER

Left: Portrait of a miniature main line, as Capt Howey always intended the RHDR to be. Only the driver and the fence posts give the scale away.
A. R. W. Crowhurst

Above: Night departure from Hythe. No 9 *Winston Churchill*, originally named *Dr Syn* until 1948.

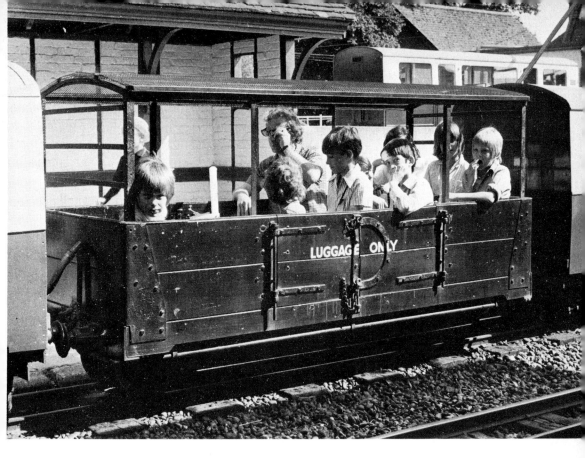

Top left: In many ways the railways remain as they always have been. *Green Goddess* is the original Pacific which went on trial to Ravenglass in 1925, and Dungeness lighthouse is equally unchanged, although it has been superseded by a later structure avoiding the nuclear power station which has been built nearby.
A. W. R. Crowhurst

Left: 4-6-2 No 10 *Dr Syn* (until 1949 named *Black Prince*) makes a steamy departure from Hythe with steam cocks wide open. *RHDR*

Above: It is remarkable how some people classify their children! *RHDR*

Overleaf: New facilities are provided to cater for additional traffic, in this case a passing loop at Maddieson's Camp, on the otherwise single line section from New Romney to Dungeness. *RHDR*

Above: Elsewhere, new railways are being laid down as additional attractions at country houses, or as in the case of the 18in gauge Bicton Woodland Railway to provide an easy means for visitors to appreciate a famous 18th century garden. How Sir Arthur Heywood would have smiled! *Woolwich*, an 0-4-0T from the shop railway at Woolwich, on the opening train of the Lakeside extension at Bicton in 1976.
Bicton Woodland Railway

Top right: The estate railway in the 1970s is a tourist pleasure line. Mostly, former industrial equipment has been refurbished for further use on passenger work, but although open to the public they are not common carrier public railways in the accepted sense. In effect they are like short miniature railways which happen to use full size narrow gauge locomotives and stock. This is the line at Knebworth House, of 2ft gauge, with Hunslet 0-4-0ST No 1 of 1922.
P. R. Foster

Right: Lincolnshire Coast Light Railway train leaving North End Land terminus behind *Jurassic*. The two coaches came from the Ashover, and the railway also owns the Sand Hutton saloon. This line is unusual among the completely new narrow gauge railways in that it is a public line — and not part of an estate.
LCLR

Railway	Gauge	Location		Chronology
Alford & Sutton Tramway	2ft 6in	Alford -Sutton	7 miles	Common Carrier 1884-1889
Ashover Light Railway	1ft 11 5/8in	Clay Cross -Ashover	7¼ miles	Freight 1924 Common Carrier 1925-1936 Freight 1936-1950
Duffield Bank Railway	1ft 3in	Duffield Bank Estate	c.1 mile	Demonstration line 1875-1916
Eaton Railway	1ft 8in	Balderton -Eaton Hall Belgrave Lodge Jn — Cuckoo's Nest	3 miles ¾ mile	Estate Railway 1896-1946
Leek & Manifold Light Railway	2ft 6in	Waterhouses- Hulme End	8¼ miles	Common Carrier 1904-1934
Lynton & Barnstaple Railway	1ft 11½in	Barnstaple -Lynton	19¼ miles	Common Carrier 1898-1935
Ravenglass & Eskdale Railway	(1) 3ft 0in	Ravenglass -Boot	67/8 miles	Freight 1875 Common Carrier 1876-1908 Freight 1908-1913 (intermittent)
	(2) 1ft 3in	Ravenglass -Dalegarth	67/8 miles	Common Carrier 1915-1952 Tourist 1952-

Locomotives	Bibliography References	Notes	Society Address
No 1 0-4-0 Tram Black Hawthorn, 1883 No 2 0-4-0 Tram Merryweather, 1884 No 3 0-4-0 Tram Dick Kerr, 1885	8		
Hummy, Guy (1st), *Joan, Peggy, Guy* (2nd), *Bridget* 4-6-0T, Baldwin 1916/1917	13		
Effie 0-4-0T, Duffield 1875 *Ella* 0-6-0T Duffield 1881 *Muriel* 0-8-0T Duffield 1894	4, 10	*Ella, Muriel* to Ravenglass & Eskdale 1917	
Katie 0-4-0T Duffield 1896 *Shelagh* (later *Katie*) 0-6-0T Duffield 1904 *Ursula,* 0-6-0T Duffield 1916	4, 10	*Katie* to Ravenglass & Eskdale 1916	
E. R. Calthrop. J. B. Earle 2-6-4T, Kitson, 1904	11		
Yeo, Exe, Taw, 2-6-2T, Manning-Wardle 1897 *Lyn,* 2-4-2T, Baldwin 1898 *Lew,* 2-6-2T, Manning-Wardle, 1925 *Devon,* 0-6-0T Manning-Wardle, 1875 *Nabb Gill,* 0-6-0T Manning-Wardle, 1876	2, 3 14 5, 7, 12		
Sans Pareil, 4-4-2, Bassett-Lowke, 1912 *Colossus,* 4-6-2, Bassett-Lowke, 1914 *Sir Aubrey Brocklebank* 4-6-2, Hunt, 1919 *River Esk,* 2-8-2, Davey Paxman, 1923 *River Irt,* 0-8-2, Ravenglass rebuild of *Muriel,* 1927 *River Mite* (1), 4-6-0+0-6-4, Ravenglass rebuild 1928 *River Mite* (2), 2-8-2, Clarkson, 1966 *Northern Rock,* 2-6-2, Ravenglass, 1976 Also *Ella, Muriel* ex Duffield Bank, *Katie* ex Eaton Railway	5, 7, 12		Ravenglass & Eskdale Railway Preservation Society 6 Orchard Road Ulverston Cumbria LA12 9QN

Railway	Gauge	Location		Chronology
Romney Hythe & Dymchurch Light Railway	1ft 3in	Hythe -Dungerness	13¾ miles	Common Carrier 1927-
Rye & Camber Tramway	3ft 0in	Rye- Camber	2½ miles	Common Carrier 1895-1939
Sand Hutton Light Railway	1ft 6in	Warhill- Barnby House White Sike Jn -Claxton	5 miles 1½ miles	Freight 1922 Common Carrier 1923-1932
Southwold Railway	3ft 0in	Halesworth -Southwold	8½ miles	Common Carrier 1879-1929
Wolverton & Stony Stratford Tramway	3ft 6in	Wolverton -Deanshanger	4½ miles	Common Carrier 1886-1926

Locomotives	Bibliography References	Notes	Society Address
1, *Green Goddess* 2 *Northern Chief,* 4-6-2, Davey Paxman 1925 3, *Southern Maid* 7, *Typhoon* 8, *Hurricane,* 4-6-2, Davey Paxman, 1927 4, *The Bug,* 0-4-0TT, Krauss, 1926 5, *Hercules* 6, *Sampson,* 4-8-2, Davey Paxman 1927 9, *Winston Churchill* (originally *Dr Syn*) 10, *Dr Syn* (originally *Black Prince*), 4-6-2, Yorkshire Engine 1931 *Black Prince,* 4-6-2 Krauss, 1937	6	The Railway is a public company and details of shareholding can be obtained from the RHDR, New Romney, Kent	Romney Hythe & Dymchurch Railway Association Light Railway Station, New Romney, Kent
Camber 2-4-0T, Bagnall, 1895 *Victoria,* 2-4-0T, Bagnall, 1897	—		
Esme, No 2, No 3, No 4 0-4-0WT, Hunslet 1916/1917	9		
Southwold, Halesworth, Blyth, 2-4-0T, Sharp Stewart, 1879 *Southwold,* 2-4-2T, Sharp Stewart, 1893 *Wenhaston,* 0-6-2T, Manning Wardle, 1916	1, 15		
Three 0-4-0Tram, Krauss, 1886 Two 0-4-0Tram, Green, ?? One 0-4-0Tram, Brown, ?? One 0-4-0ST, Bagnall, 1922	—		

River Irt leaves Ravenglass in 1972. The Ravenglass came under new management in 1960, and today is professionally run with the backing of an enthusiast society. The railway has moved away from the miniature image of the last 50 years and towards narrow gauge practice. However its first new locomotive, the second *River Mite*, seen through the spectacle plate on the shed road to the right, was built using the engine parts from *River Esk's* unsuccessful powered 0-8-0 tender and so is a scale size, inside-frame miniature locomotive like *River Esk*.   *R&ER*

ACKNOWLEDGEMENTS

The author acknowledges with gratitude the photographers and companies whose views are individually noted in the captions.

BIBLIOGRAPHY

1 Barrett, Jenkins, A. *Memories of the Southwold Railway.* F. Jenkins, 1964.
2 Brown, G. A., Prideaux, J. D. C. A., Radcliffe, H. G. *The Lynton & Barnstaple Railway.* David & Charles, 1964.
3 Catchpole, L. T. *The Lynton & Barnstaple Railway.* Oakwood, 1936.
4 Clayton, H. *The Duffield Bank and Eaton Railways.* Oakwood, 1968.
5 Davies, W. J. K. *The Ravenglass & Eskdale Railway.* David & Charles, 1968.
6 Davies, W. J. K. *The Romney, Hythe & Dymchurch Railway.* David & Charles, 1975.
7 Davies, W. J. K. (ed.) *The Ratty Bedside-Book.* Ravenglass & Eskdale Railway, 1975.
8 Dow, G. *The Alford & Sutton Tramway.* Oakwood.
9 Harley, K. E. *The Sand Hutton Light Railway.* Narrow Gauge Railway Society, 1964.
10 Heywood, Sir Arthur Percival. *Minimum Gauge Railways.* Privately published, 1898.
11 'Manifold'. *The Leek & Manifold Light Railway.* Henstock, 1955.
12 McGowan Gradon, W. *Ratty: A History of the Ravenglass & Eskdale Railway.* Privately published, 1947.
13 Plant, K. P. *The Ashover Light Railway.* Oakwood, 1965.
14 Prideaux, J. D. C. A. *Lynton & Barnstaple Railway Album.* David & Charles, 1974.
15 Taylor, A. R., Tonks, E. S. *The Southwold Railway.* Ian Allan, 1965.